STAND & WITHSTAND INTEGRITY GROUP

THE DEMAND

EDUCATION REFORM WE NEED
INITIATED BY THE STUDENTS WE LEAD

Copyright © Daniel C. Manley 2021

Layout: Stand & Withstand Integrity Group LLC
Cover Design: Dante Davis Design
Editor: Troy Butler

All rights reserved. No part of this book may be reproduced or used in any manner without the prior written permission of the copyright owner, except for the use of brief quotations in a book review.

Publisher and author make no guarantees regarding the level of success you may experience by following the recommendations and principles contained in this book, and you accept the risk that results will differ for everyone. Examples presented are exemplar results, which may not be the outcome for all, and are not intended to represent or guarantee that you will achieve similar results.

To request permissions, contact the publisher: CONTACT@standwithstand.org

Library of Congress Cataloging-in-Publication Data has been applied for.
ISBN 978-1-7369736-3-9 (Paperback)

Printed in the United States of America
First Edition October 2021

Stand & Withstand Integrity Group LLC
P.O. Box 782771
Wichita, KS 67278
STANDWITHSTAND.ORG

CONTENTS

HOW DO I USE THIS WORKBOOK? ii

INTRODUCTION: I OWE YOU 1
    WHAT DO YOU OWE ME? 2
    WRAP-UP QUESTIONS 4

CHAPTER ONE: HELP THE HELPER 6
    MORAL OF THE STORY 8
    HOW DO I GET AN EDUCATION? 8
    WHAT IS AN EDUCATION? 10
    WHY DO I GO TO SCHOOL? 12
    WHAT IS IT TO BE CERTIFIED? 14
    WHAT IS IT TO BE QUALIFIED? 16
    HOW DO TEACHERS CONTRIBUTE TO MY EDUCATION? 18
    WHY DON'T TEACHERS EDUCATE? 20
    HOW DO TEACHERS BECOME EDUCATORS? 22
    WHY PICK TEACHING OVER EDUCATING? 24
    WRAP-UP QUESTIONS 26

CHAPTER TWO: BECOME A STUDENT 28
    MORAL OF THE STORY 29
    HOW DOES A CHILD REQUIRE ANYTHING OF AN ADULT? 30
    HOW DOES A CHILD GET AN EDUCATION? 32
    WHAT IS A STUDENT? 34
    WHAT IS INTEGRITY? 36
    HOW DOES INTEGRITY IMPACT MY EDUCATION? 38
    STUDENT INTEGRITY THOUGHTS & PLEDGE 40
    WRAP-UP QUESTIONS 41

CHAPTER THREE: BE A STUDENT 42
    MORAL OF THE STORY 43
    HOW DOES A STUDENT ACT? 44
    HOW DOES A STUDENT ACT AT HOME? 46
    HOW DOES A STUDENT ACT AT SCHOOL? 48
    HOW DOES A STUDENT ACT BEFORE LEAVING SCHOOL? 50

DOES STUDENT BEHAVIOR GUARANTEE AN EDUCATION? 52
STUDENT INTEGRITY BEHAVIOR & PLEDGE 54
WRAP-UP QUESTIONS 55

CHAPTER FOUR: MAINTAIN THE STANDARD 56
MORAL OF THE STORY 57
WHO IS AT FAULT WHEN A CHILD IS UNEDUCATED? 58
WHO IS AT FAULT WHEN A STUDENT IS UNEDUCATED? 60
HOW CAN I MAKE TEACHERS RESPONSIBLE FOR EDUCATING? 62
TEACHER/EDUCATOR ASSESSMENT QUESTIONS 64
WHAT DOES SCHOOL LOOK LIKE FOR A STUDENT? 65
WHAT IS THE EDUCATIONAL VALUE CONTINUUM™? 67
EDUCATIONAL VALUE CONTINUUM™ MINIMUM FUNTIONALITY 69
EDUCATIONAL VALUE CONTINUUM™ MAXIMUM POSSIBILITY 70
HOW DO I PREVENT TEACHERS FROM WASTING MY TIME? 71
TEACHER HOMEWORK FOR PROPER PLANNING 73
STUDENT INTRODUCTION LETTER 74
WHY DO TEACHERS LIE? 76
PERSONAL PROGRESS TRACKING 78
DO I GET TO HAVE ANY FUN? 79
WRAP-UP QUESTIONS 81

CHAPTER FIVE: BE IN CONTROL 82
MORAL OF THE STORY 83
WHAT POWER DO I HAVE TO CONTROL ANYTHING? 84
WHAT IS AUTHORITY? 86
WHAT AUTHORITY DO TEACHERS HAVE? 88
WHAT AUTHORITY DO I HAVE TO USE MY POWER? 90
SELF-DISCIPLINE ASSESSMENT & PLEDGE 92
WHAT HAPPENS WHEN I AM SELF-DISCIPLINED? 93
WRAP-UP QUESTIONS 95

CHAPTER SIX: DON'T ACCEPT NO 96
MORAL OF THE STORY 97
HOW ARE TEACHERS, WHO ARE NOT EDUCATORS, HYPOCRITES? 98
EDUCATION IS THE MISSION (STATEMENTS) 100
A SYSTEM WITH INTEGRITY 102
HOW ARE TEACHERS RESPONSIBLE FOR A SYSTEM OF HYPOCRISY? 103
EDUCATIONAL VALUE CHECK QUESTIONS 105

TIME TO MAKE A DEMAND	107
HOW DO I DEMAND MY EDUCATION?	108
EDUCATIONAL GRIEVANCE FORM	110
WHAT HAPPENS AFTER I DEMAND MY EDUCATION?	111
WRAP-UP QUESTIONS	113

CHAPTER SEVEN: CALL FOR BACKUP 114

MORAL OF THE STORY	115
WHO ARE MY ALLIES?	116
ALLY STRENGTH ASSESSMENT & PLEDGE	118
HOW DO I FORM A STRONG ALLIANCE?	119
HOW WILL MY ALLIES BE THERE FOR ME?	121
HOW DO I NOT ACCEPT NO?	123
KNOW NOT TO SAY NO CHECKLIST	125
WRAP-UP QUESTIONS	126

CONCLUSION: YOU OWE YOURSELF 129

WHAT DO I OWE MYSELF?	130
WRAP-UP QUESTIONS	132

GLOSSARY OF TERMS 134

ABOUT THE AUTHOR 140

DEDICATION:

To every child who was ever told to, "Go to school and get an education," and every adult who ever said those words. Allow this book to help you to complete that conversation.

HOW DO I USE THIS WORKBOOK?

As a student, it is of the utmost importance that you possess, understand, know how to use, and benefit from materials and tools designed to assist you in pursuing an education. This booklet is to serve as a complimentary resource to *Demand It: What "Go to School and Get an Education" Really Means*. While reading that book and participating in that conversation, the thoughts, questions, and revelations you have about education, purpose, life, and your future need to be documented. You owe it to yourself to produce an artifact that serves as an introductory road map to the earliest stages of your life as a student. Let this workbook be that for you. This experience, as you read, understand, reflect, and live, has the potential to propel you into adulthood with greater clarity, preparation, and confidence. Do not take it lightly.

Philosophies:
Each chapter of the book has a main idea, expressed as an instruction, that is supported by three principles. These have been included to add emphasis and provide clarity. Your ability to know, understand, and embrace each principle better prepares you to pursue and acquire an education as a student.

Moral of the Story:
At the beginning of each *Demand It* chapter, there is a short story meant to introduce the content that follows. Use this space to reflect on the meaning of those stories and take note of the implications they hold for the chapter's overall meaning.

Notes & Questions:
As you are exposed to information in *Demand It: What "Go to School and Get an Education" Really Means*, you will develop your own thoughts, ideas, and questions as your mind seeks to explore and experience the content in a more personal way. Write them down in the space provided as notes and questions. This will allow you to reflect on and analyze them as often as you need to.

HOW DO I USE THIS WORKBOOK?

Reflect & Answer:

As you are exposed to information in *Demand It: What "Go to School and Get an Education" Really Means*, certain thoughts, ideas, and questions should cross your mind. The questions provided in this section are an example of some of them. Consider and answer them honestly to provide yourself with greater clarity. While some questions can be answered with a short, simple reply, always go as deep as you can to explore the possibility of a more profound understanding of yourself.

Summary:

You will be asked wrap-up questions at the end of each chapter. This is done to measure how well you understand the main idea of each chapter. This is to ensure that the philosophies of *Demand It: What "Go to School and Get an Education" Really Means* are being transferred from the pages of the book to the mind of the reader. Do not simply repeat and record answers to these questions word-for-word from where they have been found in the book. This space is for you to express, in everyday wording that you can relate to, the full knowledge and understanding you have of each *Demand It* principle.

INTRODUCTION:
I OWE YOU

When I tell you *I Owe You*, I am permitting you to hold me **Accountable** for knowing, understanding, and embracing the role, responsibility, and obligation of a parent. To be a parent is to act as an educator to the unlearned student that is your child. To be a parent is to provide your child with safe, appropriate space and opportunity to explore their curiosities while increasing in knowledge and experience. To be a parent is to equip and prepare your child for the successful completion of the adolescent phase of life. To assist those leading you through the educational process of life, introduce and hold them accountable to these principles:

1) Simulate School:
   Allow children to be exposed to, explore, and experience things that have a positive impact on their curiosity and benefit their maturation as they grow, develop, and become educated in the study of life.

2) Surpass Babysitting:
   Keeping children fed, clothed, sheltered, and alive are the most basic functions of the parenting role as these things do not provide the education in life necessary for advancement, success, or fulfillment; do more.

3) Schedule Childhood Graduation:
   Assist children to acquire an education in life, display maturity because of that education, and provide those responsible for their life with the confidence needed to submit responsibility over to them as this prepares children for adulthood.

2 – Introduction: I Owe You

WHAT DO YOU OWE ME?

Notes & Questions:

Simulate School / Surpass Babysitting / Schedule Childhood Graduation

Introduction: I Owe You – 3

Reflect & Answer:

<u>What do you think, how do you feel when you consider living an adult life in the future?</u>

<u>What reasons motivate you most, personally, to go to school?</u>

<u>What makes for a good, exploited worker in America?</u>

Simulate School / Surpass Babysitting / Schedule Childhood Graduation

INTRODUCTION:
Wrap-Up Questions

What does it mean to "Simulate School?"

_____
_____
_____
_____
_____
_____
_____
_____
_____

What does it mean to "Surpass Babysitting?"

_____
_____
_____
_____
_____
_____
_____
_____
_____

What does it mean to "Schedule Childhood Graduation?"

_____
_____
_____
_____
_____
_____
_____
_____
_____

Simulate School / Surpass Babysitting / Schedule Childhood Graduation

CHAPTER ONE:
HELP THE HELPER

When I tell you to *Help the Helper*, I am asking you to know, understand, and embrace the **Truth** about education, school, and the people meant to lead you through the educational process. Without your help, the uselessness of the education they offer you can leave you confused, having no understanding or direction in life. Without your help, the issues of the educational system can make the true purpose of the system an afterthought. Without your help, holding teachers accountable for educating is an impossible task for the system. To assist those leading you through the educational process, you must know, understand, and embrace these principles:

1) Admire Education:
   Respect and appreciate the fact that the next generation to acquire the immeasurable potential and intense power of a unique assortment of information they can possess, understand, use, and benefit from ensures the future success of civilization.

2) Appreciate the Environment:
   Being provided a designated area that provides safe, appropriate space and opportunity to be exposed to, explore, and experience an education makes your birthright more accessible and attainable – value those places.

3) Require Educators:
   Force the educational system to rescue teachers from their job and reposition them for their mission as this is mandatory if K-12 schools are going to fulfill their purpose.

MORAL OF THE STORY

Notes & Questions:

Reflect & Answer:
What purpose does the story serve in introducing this chapter?

Admire Education / Appreciate the Environment / Require Educators

HOW DO I GET AN EDUCATION?

Notes & Questions:

Admire Education / Appreciate the Environment / Require Educators

Reflect & Answer:

What do you feel is the expectation when people say, "Go to school and get an education?"

_____
_____
_____
_____
_____
_____
_____
_____
_____

Why do you think the word "education" has been thrown around so carelessly and so inaccurately defined?

_____
_____
_____
_____
_____
_____
_____
_____
_____

What definition for the word education did you have in your mind previously?

_____
_____
_____
_____
_____
_____
_____

Admire Education / Appreciate the Environment / Require Educators

WHAT IS AN EDUCATION?

Notes & Questions:

Reflect & Answer:

Why do you think "education" has been allowed to be so inaccurately defined for so long?

_____

What level of importance did you place on an education before?

_____

Admire Education / Appreciate the Environment / Require Educators

WHY DO I GO TO SCHOOL?

Notes & Questions:

Admire Education / Appreciate the Environment / Require Educators

Chapter One: Help The Helper – 13

Reflect & Answer:

<u>Why do you think that schools have been allowed to be as unproductive as they are when they are supposed to be so important?</u>

_____
_____
_____
_____
_____
_____
_____
_____
_____
_____
_____
_____
_____
_____

<u>Why do you think schools in suburban areas are, generally, better performing than schools in rural and urban areas?</u>

_____
_____
_____
_____
_____
_____
_____
_____
_____
_____
_____
_____
_____

Admire Education / Appreciate the Environment / Require Educators

WHAT IS IT TO BE CERTIFIED?

Notes & Questions:

Reflect & Answer:

Can you think of any people who are probably certified, but do not seem to be qualified in the area that they hold certification in?

_____
_____
_____
_____
_____
_____
_____
_____
_____
_____
_____
_____
_____

How do you think some people slip through the cracks and become certified when they are not qualified?

_____
_____
_____
_____
_____
_____
_____
_____
_____
_____
_____
_____

WHAT IS IT TO BE QUALIFIED?

Notes & Questions:

Reflect & Answer:

Why do you think people who are clearly qualified choose to not get certified at times?

What designated area would you want to be in, as often as you are required to be in traditional school, to have the space and opportunity to become educated?

Which of the five attendance levels most accurately expresses the desires you have for yourself – which one most accurately depicts your daily performance?

HOW DO TEACHERS CONTRIBUTE TO MY EDUCATION?

Notes & Questions:

Admire Education / Appreciate the Environment / Require Educators

Reflect & Answer:

What can a teacher do for an individual who is not an intellectual minor to them?

Considering the information teachers provide lessons for can always contribute to a high-quality education, why do you think so much of what people learn in school is forgotten?

Admire Education / Appreciate the Environment / Require Educators

WHY DON'T TEACHERS EDUCATE?

Notes & Questions:

Reflect & Answer:

Why do you think the number one thing instructors are supposed to do (educate) is something that they are only required to do half of (teach)?

_____
_____
_____
_____
_____
_____
_____
_____
_____
_____
_____
_____
_____
_____
_____
_____
_____
_____
_____
_____
_____
_____
_____
_____
_____
_____
_____
_____
_____

Admire Education / Appreciate the Environment / Require Educators

HOW DO TEACHERS BECOME EDUCATORS?

Notes & Questions:

Admire Education / Appreciate the Environment / Require Educators

Reflect & Answer:

Why do you think teachers fail to inform students of how and when they can use the things they learn in school in the real world?
_____
_____
_____
_____
_____
_____
_____
_____

How does it feel to be thought of as a "horse standing in front of water and not drinking?"
_____
_____
_____
_____
_____
_____
_____
_____

Would you expect that quality teaching would be enough to get students to engage and focus in class?
_____
_____
_____
_____
_____
_____
_____
_____

Admire Education / Appreciate the Environment / Require Educators

WHY PICK TEACHING OVER EDUCATING?

Notes & Questions:

Reflect & Answer:

Where do you think society should place its effort and energy to fix the issues that are now placed in the lap of the schools – are schools the best/most appropriate place?

How do you think it feels to be certified, licensed, and qualified to do one thing but judged and held responsible for how well you do another?

CHAPTER ONE:
Wrap-Up Questions

What does it mean to "Admire Education?"

_____
_____
_____
_____
_____
_____
_____
_____

What does it mean to "Appreciate the Environment?"

_____
_____
_____
_____
_____
_____
_____
_____

What does it mean to "Require Educators?"

_____
_____
_____
_____
_____
_____
_____
_____

Admire Education / Appreciate the Environment / Require Educators

CHAPTER TWO:
BECOME A STUDENT

When I tell you to *Become a Student*, I am asking you to position yourself in a place of **Righteousness** so that you can be empowered to pursue your education successfully. As a child your position is inferior, requiring you to rely on others for whatever you might need. As a student your position is superior, requiring you to take ownership and responsibility of your educational pursuit. As a student with integrity your position is solidified, stabilizing and strengthening your efforts to pursue an education. To place yourself rightfully in a position of power, you must know, understand, and embrace these principles:

1) Be Less Dangerous:
   Minimize the abundant ignorance, inexperience, and curiosity of a child that makes you a threat to yourself, a threat to others, and a threat to the possibility of acquiring an education.

2) Be More Engaged:
   Take on the pursuit of an education as a progressive task that requires you to have more responsibility than anyone else contributing to this process.

3) Have Distinct Character:
   Possess, maintain, and display student integrity to resemble the truth about education, school, and the people meant to lead you through the educational process and force the system to move.

MORAL OF THE STORY

Notes & Questions:

Reflect & Answer:
What purpose does the story serve in introducing this chapter?

Be Less Dangerous / Be More Engaged / Have Distinct Character

HOW DOES A CHILD REQUIRE ANYTHING OF AN ADULT?

Notes & Questions:

Be Less Dangerous / Be More Engaged / Have Distinct Character

Reflect & Answer:

How do you feel being a child?

How should a parent deal with the tremendous responsibility of parenting and preparing a child while also trying to protect them?

Be Less Dangerous / Be More Engaged / Have Distinct Character

HOW DOES A CHILD GET AN EDUCATION?

Notes & Questions:

Reflect & Answer:

How do you think school feels for a "student who is seriously pursuing an education" when they are forced to deal with "children in attendance at daycare?"

Be Less Dangerous / Be More Engaged / Have Distinct Character

WHAT IS A STUDENT?

Notes & Questions:

Reflect & Answer:

Describe what individuals actively engaged in the pursuit of an education look like and what they become labeled as by those less actively engaged?

How "messy" do you think America's education system is?

Be Less Dangerous / Be More Engaged / Have Distinct Character

WHAT IS INTEGRITY?

Notes & Questions:

Reflect & Answer:

Who do you know with integrity – how many people are you familiar enough with to say that they have thoughts, words, and actions that are in alignment?

Why do you think people struggle so often to maintain integrity?

Be Less Dangerous / Be More Engaged / Have Distinct Character

HOW DOES INTEGRITY IMPACT MY EDUCATION?

Notes & Questions:

Be Less Dangerous / Be More Engaged / Have Distinct Character

Reflect & Answer:

How would you describe the education system's integrity level – do they believe what they say and have actions to support it?

How brightly are you willing to shine in a dark and disingenuous place – what will it take for you to produce such a light?

Be Less Dangerous / Be More Engaged / Have Distinct Character

STUDENT INTEGRITY THOUGHTS & PLEDGE

1) An education is a unique assortment of information that one possesses (1), understands (2), knows how to use (3), and benefits from (4). I need all four components to have an education.
2) The future success of civilization depends on how well each generation can educate the next. I am the next generation, and it is my birthright to be educated.
3) The primary function of a school is to provide a safe, appropriate space and opportunity for students to have exposure to, exploration of, and experience with an education. I will not allow the other functions that schools serve to be more important than my education.
4) Every teacher is not an educator because the system does not require or hold them accountable for being so. My ability to evaluate whether my instructors are teachers or educators is critical for my educational experience.
5) Being qualified is a truer indicator of an education than being certified. I will need to be both, in most cases, to be successful in life.
6) I refuse to believe that a child's rightful place is in a seat of confinement that delays the ability and opportunity to attain power, become independent, and experience life.
7) Being a child, having someone else more responsible for my own life than I am, does not mean that I cannot be a student and accept responsibility for my own education.
8) An education must be acquired *by* me, it cannot be given *to* me.
9) The space and opportunity needed to be exposed to, explore, and experience an education are rightfully mine. I am authorized to make demands on the quality of them both.
10) Maintaining integrity as a student solidifies my right to make demands while actively engaging in the pursuit of an education.

I acknowledge that I understand the importance of embracing these beliefs and rooting them deeply in my mind as the originating thoughts that my integrity as a student will be birthed from.

_____(Signature)

Be Less Dangerous / Be More Engaged / Have Distinct Character

CHAPTER TWO:
Wrap-Up Questions

What does it mean to "Be Less Dangerous?"

_____
_____
_____
_____
_____
_____
_____
_____

What does it mean to "Be More Engaged?"

_____
_____
_____
_____
_____
_____
_____
_____

What does it mean to "Have Distinct Character?"

_____
_____
_____
_____
_____
_____
_____
_____

Be Less Dangerous / Be More Engaged / Have Distinct Character

CHAPTER THREE:
BE A STUDENT

When I tell you to *Be a Student*, I am asking you to walk in the footsteps that integrity requires of you to maintain **Peace** on your journey. The motivation you have for this journey, though abstract, must be securely in your sights. Your words and actions are concrete evidence and confirming indicators that integrity is truly possessed. Evaluating the goals and success you have will confirm how aligned you are with the integrity of a student. To walk in the footsteps that integrity requires, you must know, understand, and embrace these principles:

1) Stay Set

    Focus on your internal desire and willingness to acquire an education while fulfilling the internal and external prerequisites necessary to do so.

2) Look & Listen:

    Continuously have behaviors and conversations that bear witness to you being a student seriously pursuing an education.

3) Change & Confirm:

    Realign and establish that the position you *need* to be in is the same position you *are* in to validate your integrity and support your right to make demands on the quality of your education.

MORAL OF THE STORY

Notes & Questions:

_____
_____
_____
_____
_____
_____
_____
_____
_____
_____
_____
_____
_____
_____
_____

Reflect & Answer:
What purpose does the story serve in introducing this chapter?
_____
_____
_____
_____
_____
_____
_____
_____
_____
_____
_____
_____

Stay Set / Look & Listen / Change & Confirm

HOW DOES A STUDENT ACT?

Notes & Questions:

Stay Set / Look & Listen / Change & Confirm

Reflect & Answer:

What would those who see you often say your conduct displays a clear and present focus on – is that who you are – is that who you truly desire to be?

Stay Set / Look & Listen / Change & Confirm

HOW DOES A STUDENT ACT AT HOME?

Notes & Questions:

Stay Set / Look & Listen / Change & Confirm

Chapter Three: Be A Student – 47

Reflect & Answer:

How often would you say your readiness and preparation levels for school are different from each other – how often do you see them being the same?

When you are not at school, how much of your time, energy, and effort goes into making yourself more ready/prepared to be productive while at school?

Stay Set / Look & Listen / Change & Confirm

HOW DOES A STUDENT ACT AT SCHOOL?

Notes & Questions:

Stay Set / Look & Listen / Change & Confirm

Reflect & Answer:

How often have you seen, heard, or experienced school as a prison sentence rather than a designated area providing educational space and opportunity?

_____
_____
_____
_____
_____
_____
_____
_____
_____
_____
_____
_____

What personal principles are your behaviors publicizing to others when you are at school?

_____
_____
_____
_____
_____
_____
_____
_____
_____
_____
_____
_____

Stay Set / Look & Listen / Change & Confirm

HOW DOES A STUDENT ACT BEFORE LEAVING SCHOOL?

Notes & Questions:

Stay Set / Look & Listen / Change & Confirm

Reflect & Answer:

How do you typically gauge and/or decide if you have had a "successful" day at school – what do you need to have received or experienced in order to consider it so?

Stay Set / Look & Listen / Change & Confirm

DOES STUDENT BEHAVIOR GUARANTEE AN EDUCATION?

Notes & Questions:

Stay Set / Look & Listen / Change & Confirm

Chapter Three: Be A Student

Reflect & Answer:

Why do you think so many people have been allowed to walk into a place meant to provide them with an education and walk out without one?

_____
_____
_____
_____
_____
_____
_____
_____
_____
_____
_____
_____
_____
_____
_____
_____

How do you intend to make sure you are not one of those people?

_____
_____
_____
_____
_____
_____
_____
_____
_____
_____
_____
_____
_____
_____
_____

Stay Set / Look & Listen / Change & Confirm

STUDENT INTEGRITY BEHAVIOR & PLEDGE

1) I embrace the mentality, ideas, and beliefs that serve as the originating thoughts for my student integrity to be birthed from.

2) I have actions and behaviors that consistently display a clear and present focus on the education I am pursuing.

3) I have actions and behaviors that consistently display a readiness and preparation to attend and actively engage while at school.

4) I have actions and behaviors that consistently display a willingness to be challenged and overcome challenges as they arise.

5) I have actions and behaviors that consistently display an unwillingness to leave school without confidence that progress is being made toward my goals.

6) I speak words and have conversations that cause others to say, "That sounds like a student seriously pursuing an education."

7) I display behaviors and demonstrate actions that cause others to say, "That looks like a student seriously pursuing an education."

8) I evaluate the educational space and opportunities that I am given.

9) I take inventory of what information (1), understanding (2), uses (3), and benefits (4) I acquire from my educational experiences.

10) I establish where that inventory belongs on the Educational Value Continuum™.

I acknowledge that I understand the importance of these tasks and continually assessing my behaviors against them as they are the corresponding actions to the originating thoughts that my integrity as a student will be birthed from.

_____(Signature)

Stay Set / Look & Listen / Change & Confirm

CHAPTER THREE:
Wrap-Up Questions

What does it mean to "Stay Set?"

_____
_____
_____
_____
_____
_____
_____

What does it mean to "Look & Listen?"

_____
_____
_____
_____
_____
_____
_____

What does it mean to "Change & Confirm?"

_____
_____
_____
_____
_____
_____
_____

Stay Set / Look & Listen / Change & Confirm

CHAPTER FOUR:
MAINTAIN THE STANDARD

When I tell you to *Maintain the Standard*, I am asking you to have **Faith** that your beliefs, position, and integrity are the best tools to measure how well your educational pursuit is going. When you assess your teachers and require them to work, you are helping them to align with the purpose of school. When you chart the educational value of the work you are given, you are holding teachers accountable for being the educators the system says it wants. When you assess your work and honestly evaluate the quality of it, you are eliminating the possibility of being given a false sense of your abilities. To measure how well your educational pursuit is going, you must know, understand, and embrace these principles:

1) Make Them Work:
   Require your teachers to answer questions that are deep and broad in a positive, confident, and clear way to validate their acceptance of the responsibility of educating.

2) Know the Value:
   Challenge the worth of assignments, task, and experiences that cannot be tracked and recorded as useful and beneficial as they are counterproductive and offer only half of an education.

3) Monitor Your Progress:
   Track your own educational journey and require others to provide evidence that supports their assessment claims to prevent them from designing an experience for you that is missing a complete education.

MORAL OF THE STORY

Notes & Questions:

Reflect & Answer:
What purpose does the story serve in introducing this chapter?

WHO IS AT FAULT WHEN A CHILD IS UNEDUCATED?

Notes & Questions:

Reflect & Answer:

What does an appropriately sliced "blame pie" look like for an uneducated child (who gets what percentage of the pie – parents, society, schools, child, whoever)?

WHO IS AT FAULT WHEN A STUDENT IS UNEDUCATED?

Notes & Questions:

Make Them Work / Know the Value / Track Your Progress

Reflect & Answer:

What does an appropriately sliced "blame pie" look like for an uneducated student (who gets what percentage of the pie – parents, society, schools, student, whoever)?

HOW CAN I MAKE TEACHERS RESPONSIBLE FOR EDUCATING?

Notes & Questions:

Make Them Work / Know the Value / Track Your Progress

Reflect & Answer:

Why/how is it that what seems plain and obvious (the difference between teaching/teachers and educating/educators) has been a problem for the education system for so long?
_____
_____
_____
_____
_____
_____
_____
_____

Think about your experience and compare/contrast those individuals that you believe to be teachers with others that are clearly educators in your mind.
_____
_____
_____
_____
_____
_____
_____
_____

Why do you think teachers would find it difficult to be questioned by a young person with these types of questions?
_____
_____
_____
_____
_____
_____
_____

TEACHER/EDUCATOR ASSESSMENT QUESTIONS

Asking these questions will inform you whether you are being led by a teacher or an educator. If, when, and how you receive a response from this line of questioning will reveal to you the caliber of instructor you are dealing with:

1. What intentions do you have for me in this class?
   a) What goals should I reach by the end of the year?
   b) How will you measure my progress from now until then?
   c) Will I be offered an education in full or in part?

2. Outside of your credentials and certificates, what qualities make you an effective educator?
   a) What, unique, is being offered in your class?
   b) What experience do you bring to class that qualify you to teach this content so that it has a lasting impression on me?
   c) How would you rate yourself as an educator?

3. Is the focus of your classroom management discipline, traditional school, or providing me with the best educational environment?
   a) What are your reasons for the seating arrangement and my allowance/disallowance of movement?
   b) How often am I allowed to interact, engage, and work with others?
   c) When I "sit-and-get," how good is that which I will be getting?

Make Them Work / Know the Value / Track Your Progress

Chapter Four: Maintain The Standard – 65

WHAT DOES SCHOOL LOOK LIKE FOR A STUDENT?

Notes & Questions:

Make Them Work / Know the Value / Track Your Progress

Reflect & Answer:

What memories do you have of experiencing school in the way it was always meant to be experienced?

How much work do you anticipate doing to support your declaration that you are a student seriously pursuing an education – do you intend on making such a declaration?

Make Them Work / Know the Value / Track Your Progress

WHAT IS THE EDUCATIONAL VALUE CONTINUUM™?

Notes & Questions:

Chapter Four: Maintain The Standard

Reflect & Answer:

How much sense does it make for a student to rely on scores and grades, that do not fully express what is being learned, to provide understanding of and track the education that they are supposed to be receiving?

How much more likely would you be to take classes if you knew how using information from those classes could benefit you personally?

Make Them Work / Know the Value / Track Your Progress

EDUCATIONAL VALUE CONTINUUM™

Minimum Functionality:

On the most basic level, what purpose does the study of this subject and support material serve in my life (now or in the foreseeable future) that benefits me directly?

1) **Ability** – offers the power or capability to do.
   Learners Say: "I now know how to ____ and can ____."

2) **Skill** – raises the level and proficiency of an ability already possessed.
   Learners Say: "I am now better at ____."

3) **Vocation** – develops the understanding of a certain job, profession, or business.
   Learners Say: "I now know (what / what a) ____ (are / is) and (do / does)."

4) **Relationship** – develops the understanding of human connection, interaction, and involvement.
   Learners Say: "I can now relate better to ____ because of ____."

5) **Mentality** – challenges, changes, composes, or confirms personal perspectives on life or the world.
   Learners Say: "My ideas about ____ (are now / have been) ____ due to ____."

6) **Mental Exercise** – works, conditions, or trains the brain for better overall functionality.
   Learners Say: "I am able (to / to do) ____ (better / more) because I have exercised my mind."

7) **Muscle Memory** – works, conditions, or trains the physical body for better overall functionality.
   Learners Say: "I am able (to / to do) ____ (better / more) because I have exercised my body."

8) **Practice** – provides time and opportunity to raise competence or effectiveness of an ability.
   Learners Say: "I worked to improve my ____ by doing ____."

9) **Training** – provides purposeful, more disciplined, focused, and intensive practice of a specific ability to become more skilled.
   Learners Say: "I worked to improve my ____ by doing ____."

10) **Experience** – encountering and becoming more familiar in order to raise one's awareness or aptitude.
    Learners Say: "I spent time ____ to be (better / more) ____ (at / with / of) ____."

Make Them Work / Know the Value / Track Your Progress

EDUCATIONAL VALUE CONTINUUM™

Maximum Possibility:
At the most accomplished and advanced level, what purpose could the study of this subject and support material(s) serve in my life and what beneficial position could it ultimately land me in?

1) **Motivation** – creates or causes a reason to act.
   Learners Say: "I now have a (desire / stronger desire) to ____."
2) **Inspiration** – sparks or ignites an internal motivation.
   Learners Say: "I feel ____ compelling me to ____."
3) **Higher Education** – instills the desire to pursue an education past the high school level.
   Learners Say: "I want to go to ____ and study ____ (to / so that) ____."
4) **Career** – instills the desire to pursue a specific profession or occupation.
   Learners Say: "I want to (be a / work for) ____ so that I can ____."
5) **Dream** – instills the desire to pursue a grandiose goal, passion, or vision.
   Learners Say: "I want (to / to be) ____ and one day ____."
6) **Invention** – stimulates the imagination to create something that did not exist previously.
   Learners Say: "I want to create (a / the) ____ that (can / will) ____."
7) **Innovation** – stimulates the imagination to create something newer than the already established.
   Learners Say: "I want to improve ____ so that (it / it can) ____."
8) **Non-Profit** – motivates one to establish, develop, and pursue goals meant to provide a public service or benefit.
   Learners Say: "I want to help ____ so they will be able to ____."
9) **Fortune-500** – motivates one to establish, develop, and pursue goals meant to gain significant financial wealth.
   Learners Say: "I want to become ____ and acquire ____."
10) **Superhero** – motivates one to establish, develop, and pursue goals meant to effect positive change on the largest possible scale.
    Learners Say: "I want to impact and improve ____ by ____."

Make Them Work / Know the Value / Track Your Progress

HOW DO I PREVENT TEACHERS FROM WASTING MY TIME?

Notes & Questions:

Make Them Work / Know the Value / Track Your Progress

Reflect & Answer:

<u>Unless you require your teachers to be educators, they are going to waste your time – how do you feel about that?</u>

_____
_____
_____
_____
_____
_____
_____
_____
_____
_____
_____
_____
_____

<u>How does it feel to know that you, as a student, are also responsible for keeping the teacher on task?</u>

_____
_____
_____
_____
_____
_____
_____
_____
_____
_____
_____
_____
_____
_____
_____

Make Them Work / Know the Value / Track Your Progress

TEACHER HOMEWORK FOR PROPER PLANNING

To ensure that the best opportunities for a high-quality education are being offered to you regularly, and the information you are being provided with fits somewhere on the Educational Value Continuum™, your teachers should be able to answer these questions. Their ability to answer these questions positively, confidently, and clearly are evidence that they have accepted the responsibility of educating you:

1) What does this lesson offer me that I can use?
   a) How can I use and benefit from this lesson's information in the real-world?
   b) Does this information benefit me educationally, or is it just work?
   c) What is the least/most I could gain from this lesson to support me living a more fulfilled life?

2) How similar/different is the experience I will have compared to what wealthier students at a more respected school would get?
   a) Would you plan or teach this lesson differently for wealthier students?
   b) Would you plan or teach this lesson differently at a more respected school?
   c) Are these learning opportunities less than, greater than, or equal to what would be provided to wealthy families at an expensive private school?

3) Have you perfected this lesson?
   a) Does this lesson meet at least 90% of your goals with at least 90% of your audience at least 90% of the time?
   b) Do you believe you could teach this lesson anytime, anywhere, to anybody and accomplish the goals you planned for?
   c) Why do you teach this lesson the way that you do?

Make Them Work / Know the Value / Track Your Progress

STUDENT INTRODUCTION LETTER

At the earliest possible moment, instructors' whose classes you are assigned to need to be made aware of who you are and that their time with you is not to be taken lightly. It needs to be established that strategic planning is necessary to work with you as a student in the classroom. An email can be composed by you or a parent as an introduction to communicate your intentions as a student:

Mr. or Ms. (Teacher's Last Name),

    I am contacting you to introduce (myself / my child) and begin the educational process for the (Year of Attendance) school year. (My / Their) name is (Student's First and Last Name), and (I am / they are) a student who is serious about pursuing an education at school with you as my educator. (I am / They are) scheduled to be in your (Class Hour & Class Subject) class, and (I / we) would like to know a bit more about who (I / we) will be working with.

    To be clear, when I say student, I am saying "one who is actively engaged in the pursuit of an education." What I mean by education is "a unique assortment of information that one possesses, understands, knows how to use, and benefits from." When I say school, I mean "a designated area that provides space and opportunity to be exposed to, explore, and experience an education." By calling you an educator, I expect that you will "carefully plan, teach, and complete lessons intentionally designed to assist me in attaining the education I pursue." An educator, as I have been informed, is an individual who should be able to answer questions that are "deep and broad in a positive, confident, and clear way." These are the questions that I would like for you to consider:

1) <u>What intentions do you have for me in this class?</u>
   a. What goals should I reach by the end of the year?
   b. How will you measure my progress from now until then?
   c. Will I be offered an education in full or in part?

2. <u>Outside of your credentials and certificates, what qualities make you an effective educator?</u>
   a. What, unique, is being offered in your class?
   b. What experience do you bring to class that qualify you to teach this content so that it has a lasting impression on me?
   c. How would you rate yourself as an educator?

Make Them Work / Know the Value / Track Your Progress

3. Is the focus of your classroom management discipline, traditional school, or providing me with the best educational environment?
   a. What are your reasons for the seating arrangement and my allowance/disallowance of movement?
   b. How often am I allowed to interact, engage, and work with others?
   c. When I "sit-and-get," how good is that which I will be getting?

I was also informed that your consideration of these questions can be beneficial when planning:

1) What does this lesson offer me that I can use?
   a) How can I use and benefit from this lesson's information in the real-world?
   b) Does this information benefit me educationally, or is it just work?
   c) What is the least/most I could gain from this lesson to support me living a more fulfilled life?

2) How similar/different is the experience I will have compared to what wealthier students at a more respected school would get?
   a) Would you plan or teach this lesson differently for wealthier students?
   b) Would you plan or teach this lesson differently at a more respected school?
   c) Are these learning opportunities less than, greater than, or equal to what would be provided to wealthy families at an expensive private school?

3) Have you perfected this lesson?
   a) Does this lesson meet at least 90% of your goals with at least 90% of your audience at least 90% of the time?
   b) Do you believe you could teach this lesson anytime, anywhere, to anybody and accomplish the goals you planned for?
   c) Why do you teach this lesson the way that you do?

I am not requesting that your response have answers to all of these questions. I have included them for your consideration, reflection, and planning. I appreciate the time, energy, and resources that you will be investing in (me / my child) this year to help make (my / their) educational pursuit more productive and successful. Have a good day and thank you for taking the time to read this message.

I look forward to your response.

(Your First & Last Name)

Make Them Work / Know the Value / Track Your Progress

WHY DO TEACHERS LIE?

Notes & Questions:

Reflect & Answer:

Consider working for a prize that is incredibly difficult to attain – would you rather be falsely praised for reaching a subpar standard, or have peace and confidence knowing that whatever you attain is valid?

_____
_____
_____
_____
_____
_____
_____
_____

Should you be flattered or feel like you are being set-up by someone trying to convince you that you are better than you know you are?

_____
_____
_____
_____
_____
_____
_____

How do you think it feels trying to perform at a level that you are not ready or prepared for?

_____
_____
_____
_____
_____
_____
_____
_____

Make Them Work / Know the Value / Track Your Progress

PERSONAL PROGRESS TRACKING

Until you can be sure these questions are being answered honestly, confidently, and with detailed feedback on a regular basis, you need to be skeptical of any praise, compliment, assessment score, or grade you receive:

1) Is my completion of this assignment evidence that I have completed a phase of learning that supports my education?
    a) Could I have completed this assignment without completing the learning that was meant to be paired with it?
    b) Could I have completed the learning meant to be paired with this assignment without completing the assignment?
    c) Can I see how this assignment supports my pursuit of an education or does it just seem like work?

2) What is the grade on this assignment really mean?
    a) Is this grade a true representation of me or the quality of my work?
        i) Did I really need to be or do "excellent" to receive an 'A' grade?
        ii) Did I really need to be or do something "failure like" to receive an 'F' grade?
    b) Does this grade mean I am making progress in my educational pursuit?
    c) Did I receive this grade simply because I did the work?

3) Does this grade have an absolute value?
    a) How much of this grade is a measure of my effort?
    b) How much of this grade is measuring the strength of my education?
    c) How much of this grade is a measure of something that is not educational?

Make Them Work / Know the Value / Track Your Progress

DO I GET TO HAVE ANY FUN?

Notes & Questions:

Make Them Work / Know the Value / Track Your Progress

Reflect & Answer:

<u>When you think of "fun" what comes to mind – could those things be broken down to simple enjoyment?</u>

<u>How much of a factor should fun be when you are working to prepare yourself for a successful life?</u>

<u>Can you think of examples where people substitute long-term success and fulfillment for short-term enjoyment?</u>

CHAPTER FOUR:
Wrap-Up Questions

What does it mean to "Make Them Work?"

_____
_____
_____
_____
_____
_____
_____
_____

What does it mean to "Know the Value?"

_____
_____
_____
_____
_____
_____
_____
_____

What does it mean to "Monitor Your Progress?"

_____
_____
_____
_____
_____
_____
_____
_____

Make Them Work / Know the Value / Track Your Progress

CHAPTER FIVE:
BE IN CONTROL

When I tell you to *Be in Control*, I am asking you to preserve the **Salvation** of your school experience as a student. The power you have makes the possibility of controlling your entire life a reality for you. This reality can only be experienced once righteous authority trust you to use that power – once they give you the authority. When this happens, if you display the self-discipline necessary for it to happen, the only thing that can stop you is your imagination. To preserve the possibility of making your imagination your reality, you must know, understand, and embrace these principles:

1) Understand Power:
   Recognize and respect the fact that a child exercising their ability to do everything they have the capability of doing, can very easily result in danger, destruction, and death.

2) Honor Righteous Authority
   Prove that you have the education required to use power appropriately, efficiently, and with a high probability of success to be authorized to use it.

3) Show Restraint
   Self-discipline dictates how much authority can be given to a child looking to become a student and operate as righteous authority over their own educational pursuit; develop it.

MORAL OF THE STORY

Notes & Questions:

Reflect & Answer:
What purpose does the story serve in introducing this chapter?

WHAT POWER DO I HAVE TO CONTROL ANYTHING?

Notes & Questions:

Understand Power / Honor Righteous Authority / Show Restraint

Reflect & Answer:

Who and/or what makes you feel as though you are powerless?

Do you remember what it felt like to discover, for the first time, that you could do something you did not have the power to do previously?

Understand Power / Honor Righteous Authority / Show Restraint

WHAT IS AUTHORITY?

Notes & Questions:

Reflect & Answer:

Is there any particular permission that you look forward to having more than others – what will it take for you to receive this permission – who can grant it to you?

_____
_____
_____
_____
_____
_____
_____
_____
_____
_____
_____
_____
_____
_____

What authority figures do you see as being most righteous; what is it about them that makes you view them this way – what must they see in you to consider you to be in alignment with them?

_____
_____
_____
_____
_____
_____
_____
_____
_____
_____
_____
_____
_____
_____

Understand Power / Honor Righteous Authority / Show Restraint

WHAT AUTHORITY DO TEACHERS HAVE?

Notes & Questions:

Understand Power / Honor Righteous Authority / Show Restraint

Reflect & Answer:

How does it look, sound, and/or feel when a teacher overexerts their control outside of the scope of their authority – why do young people allow it to happen?

_____
_____
_____
_____
_____
_____
_____

How often do you feel as though you are trusted to do anything in a classroom that a teacher did not give you clear instructions to do?

_____
_____
_____
_____
_____
_____
_____

Do your classes, most often, feel like hostage situations where any movement might just cost you something – why or why not?

_____
_____
_____
_____
_____
_____
_____
_____
_____

Understand Power / Honor Righteous Authority / Show Restraint

WHAT AUTHORITY DO I HAVE TO USE MY POWER?

Notes & Questions:

Reflect & Answer:

<u>Why is it so difficult to master control over oneself – what are the things that get in the way of doing this appropriately and efficiently with a high probability of success?</u>

SELF-DISCIPLINE ASSESSMENT & PLEDGE

Self-discipline, displaying to righteous authority that you are qualified to be an authority over your own life, also gives you permission to make demands on your education when you see that your pursuit is not being supported. To properly gauge the level of self-discipline you have, ask yourself these questions when trying to decide whether to move forward with any decision:

1) Do I have the power to do this thing?
2) Do I have the education required to do this thing appropriately and efficiently with a high probability of success?
3) What righteous authority (person or document) do I need to be aligned with to have authority over this matter?
4) Has it been clearly established that I have direct authority to do this thing?
5) What is the source (person or document) of that authority?
6) Am I comfortable and confident using authority that has not been clearly established as mine?
7) What righteous authority (person or document) gives me the comfort and confidence to move forward without it?
8) Does my doing this thing raise the quality and potential of my educational experience?

I acknowledge that I understand the importance of acquiring the education required to do things appropriately and efficiently with a high probability of success. I understand that displaying such things to righteous authority is what will portray me as self-disciplined, and that self-discipline is what gives me control over my own life.

_____(Signature)

Understand Power / Honor Righteous Authority / Show Restraint

WHAT HAPPENS WHEN I AM SELF-DISCIPLINED?

Notes & Questions:

Reflect & Answer:

Who are the most disciplined people you know?

What is it about these people that says to you that they are disciplined?

What difficulties do you see coming with being righteous authority over your own educational pursuit?

CHAPTER FIVE:
Wrap-Up Questions

What does it mean to "Understand Power?"

_____
_____
_____
_____
_____
_____
_____
_____

What does it mean to "Honor Righteous Authority?"

_____
_____
_____
_____
_____
_____
_____
_____

What does it mean to "Show Restraint?"

_____
_____
_____
_____
_____
_____
_____
_____

Understand Power / Honor Righteous Authority / Show Restraint

CHAPTER SIX:
DON'T ACCEPT NO

When I tell you *Don't Accept No*, I am asking you to allow a **Spirit** to rest in you that makes you equal to every other figure in history that refused to settle for less. This force would not allow the inconsistent character of another to be a consistent disruption in their educational pursuit. This force would stand firm and require the delivery of the high-quality educational opportunity that is rightfully theirs. Denying this force will not extinguish a flame, but fuel it to burn at extraordinary temperatures. To allow yourself to become equal with this force, you must know, understand, and embrace these principles:

1) Expose Hypocrisy
   Someone being allowed to diminish the quality of educational service you receive makes the successful completion of an educational pursuit improbable and/or impossible; report any effort to do so with an official complaint.

2) File a Grievance
   An official complaint meant to correct an issue working against your educational pursuit needs to:
   - Include the details of hypocrisy.
   - Clearly communicate a reasonable solution
   - Include a direct plan of action for those responsible for correcting the issue.
   - Include a projected timetable for the resolution of the grievance.

3) Be Honorable
   Respectability, dignity, and grace support your position and goal while revealing that the true purpose of your complaint is to acquire a better education; be careful to display each consistently.

MORAL OF THE STORY

Notes & Questions:

_____
_____
_____
_____
_____
_____
_____
_____
_____
_____
_____
_____
_____
_____
_____
_____

Reflect & Answer:
What purpose does the story serve in introducing this chapter?

_____
_____
_____
_____
_____
_____
_____
_____
_____
_____
_____
_____
_____

Expose Hypocrisy / File A Grievance / Be Honorable

HOW ARE TEACHERS, WHO ARE NOT EDUCATORS, HYPOCRITES?

Notes & Questions:

Reflect & Answer:

<u>What reasons could you imagine for a teacher to be made aware of these insights and continue to teach rather than educate?</u>

_____
_____
_____
_____
_____
_____
_____
_____
_____
_____
_____
_____
_____
_____
_____
_____
_____
_____
_____
_____
_____
_____
_____
_____
_____
_____
_____
_____

Expose Hypocrisy / File A Grievance / Be Honorable

EDUCATION IS THE MISSION

Knowing the mission statements, vision statements, and core values of your state, district, and building are mandatory if you plan on holding them accountable. If you make *their* words traps for them to become entangled in, there is no way for them to go against themselves when you point out inconsistencies in the outcome of your experience. Individual teacher's syllabi are to be given the same attention. These are not just words on a page, these are promises being made about the overall quality of your educational experience:

Your **State's** Mission & Vision Statements and/or Other Promises:
_____
_____
_____
_____
_____

Your **District's** Mission & Vision Statements and/or Other Promises:
_____
_____
_____
_____
_____

Your **School's** Mission & Vision Statements and/or Other Promises:
_____
_____
_____
_____
_____
_____

Your **Teacher's** Mission & Vision Statements and/or Other Promises:
_____
_____
_____
_____

Expose Hypocrisy / File A Grievance / Be Honorable

Your **Teacher's** Mission & Vision Statements and/or Other Promises:
_____
_____
_____

Your **Teacher's** Mission & Vision Statements and/or Other Promises:
_____
_____
_____

Your **Teacher's** Mission & Vision Statements and/or Other Promises:
_____
_____
_____

Your **Teacher's** Mission & Vision Statements and/or Other Promises:
_____
_____
_____

Your **Teacher's** Mission & Vision Statements and/or Other Promises:
_____
_____
_____

Your **Teacher's** Mission & Vision Statements and/or Other Promises:
_____
_____
_____

Your **Teacher's** Mission & Vision Statements and/or Other Promises:
_____
_____
_____

Expose Hypocrisy / File A Grievance / Be Honorable

A SYSTEM WITH INTEGRITY

An education system void of hypocrisy would be a system with thoughts, words, and actions that all resemble the same thing. Being so, the individual contributors to that system would be allied, aligned, and consistent in expressing and executing their united mission. Such a system, having "education" as their goal and purpose, would be connected in their respective missions:

School Building Mission:
"To contribute to student's discovery of purpose by providing safe, appropriate space and opportunity for exposure to, exploration of, and experience with a unique assortment of information they can possess, understand, use, and benefit from so they can pursue and acquire the education necessary to live a fulfilled life."

School Administrator Mission:
"To ensure the routine functionality of an academic institution provides students with a safe, appropriate space and opportunity for exposure to, exploration of, and experience with a unique assortment of information that they can possess, understand, use, and benefit from so they can pursue and acquire the education necessary to live a fulfilled life."

School Educator Mission:
"To, intentionally, teach lessons and plan activities that allow students to be exposed to, explore, and experience an education to provoke and support them in pursuing and acquiring the education necessary to live a fulfilled life."

School Student Mission:
"To consistently demonstrate the character and integrity needed to actively engage in the pursuit of an education in order to acquire an education and be prepared to take full responsibility for my life and livelihood before adulthood in an effort to live a fulfilled life."

Parent and/or Guardian Mission:
"To serve as an ally to both my child and the academic institution by holding them (student) accountable for the character and integrity they need in order to pursue and acquire an education, and for their (school) contribution to my child's discovery of purpose."

HOW ARE TEACHERS RESPONSIBLE FOR A SYSTEM OF HYPOCRISY?

Notes & Questions:

Reflect & Answer:

Having the educational system facilitated most by the teaching profession makes it seem as though educators and teachers are the same thing – explain how/why they are not?

_____
_____
_____
_____
_____
_____
_____
_____
_____
_____
_____
_____

Outside of the direct connection between students, teachers, and the classroom, can you think of any other reasons why teachers are at fault for the hypocrisy of the system?

_____
_____
_____
_____
_____
_____
_____
_____
_____
_____
_____
_____

EDUCATIONAL VALUE CHECK

When teachers cannot, will not, or do not tell students the uses for and benefits of the content they are teaching, they are withholding the education that is meant to be acquired. A student experiencing this hypocrisy is right to ask questions. To be exposed to, explore, and experience the functions and possibilities of a certain content, ask these questions when you recognize that the final two components of your education are missing from the classroom experience:

1) Can you help me better understand this information?
   a) Can you repeat that please?
   b) Could you give me an example please?
   c) Can you make that more real, relevant, or practical for me please?

2) How could I use this information in the real-world?
   a) Does this give me an ability that will help me in life – which ones and how?
   b) Does this help me to be more skilled in an ability that will help me in life – which ones and how?
   c) Is there a job, profession, or business that this helps me to better do or understand – which ones and how?
   d) Can this help to improve the quality of my relationships and interactions – which ones and how?
   e) Is this supposed to challenge, change, confirm, or help me to compose ideas about the world – which ones and how?
   f) Is this helping my brain to function better – which parts and how?
   g) Is this helping my body to function better – which parts and how?
   h) Am I working/practicing to improve something – what and why?
   i) Am I working/training to excel at something – what and why?
   j) Is doing this giving me experience in something that will help me – what and how?

3) How could I benefit from this information in the real-world?
   a) Is this something that could motivate me – how?

Expose Hypocrisy / File A Grievance / Be Honorable

b) Is this something that could inspire me – how?
c) Could this help me figure out if/what I want to study in college – how?
d) Could this help me figure out career paths to pursue – how and which ones?
e) Could this push me to develop/achieve a dream – how?
f) Could I use this to invent something – what and/or how?
g) Could I use this to improve something – what and/or how?
h) Could this cause me to want to help people in life – who and how?
i) Could this cause me to want to pursue wealth, affluence, and power in life – where and how?
j) Could this cause me to want to pursue a better future for humanity – how?

TIME TO MAKE A DEMAND

The uses for and benefits of the information they provide you in class are 50% of the education you look to acquire. If they fail or refuse to provide you with them, the educational process is inconsistent with the educational promise. Allowing these inconsistencies to occur repeatedly throughout a K-12 academic career, without calling them into question and resolving them, prevent students from acquiring the education they pursue. If this is the case, if this is your experience, a demand on your education most certainly needs to be made. Asking these questions will reveal to you whether or not you have good reason to make such a demand:

1) Have I understood, embraced, and adopted the mentality of a student?
2) Have I exhibited the behaviors and actions that support those beliefs?
3) Have I maintained student integrity in my pursuit of an education?
4) Have I assessed the quality of the teacher, space, and opportunity I have been offered?
5) Have I assessed the value of what I have been given to learn, work on, and experience?
6) Have I been given insufficient space and opportunity to be exposed to, explore, and experience an education?
7) Am I aware of what righteous authority says I should be receiving in my K-12 academic experience?
8) Am I aware of what this teacher says I should be receiving in my classroom experience?
9) Have I encountered contradictions and inconsistencies to what I should be receiving?
10) Have I made a reasonable attempt to get the necessary help to resolve this issue?

Expose Hypocrisy / File A Grievance / Be Honorable

HOW DO I DEMAND MY EDUCATION?

Notes & Questions:

Expose Hypocrisy / File A Grievance / Be Honorable

Reflect & Answer:

Explain the difference between complaining and filing a grievance?

Consider the biggest, most problematic conflicts that you know to have ever been resolved – what did it take for resolution to attained?

Do you have what it takes to be honorable in the midst of great conflict – what does that say about you?

Expose Hypocrisy / File A Grievance / Be Honorable

EDUCATIONAL GRIEVENCE FORM

The refusal of academic authority figures to support the educational pursuit of students by denying them adequate space and opportunity to do so is deception, fraud, and neglect. The individual most responsible for your complaint should be who you discuss the matter with first. If that conversation is unproductive/unsuccessful, then you are right to move up the hierarchy and express your issue to their superior (department chair, assistant principal, head principal, district office, school board member/committee, superintendent, local newspaper, local television network, etc.). This can, should, and will need to continue until someone recognizes how valid your concern is and helps you by correcting it:

Official Complaint:
_____
_____

Statute Disrupted:
_____
_____

Person(s) Responsible:
_____

Attempted Resolution:
_____
_____

Resolution Now Desired:
_____
_____

Expected Course of Action:

TASK	DEADLINE	DONE	INITIALS
	[Date]	☐	
	[Date]	☐	
	[Date]	☐	
	[Date]	☐	

Expose Hypocrisy / File A Grievance / Be Honorable

WHAT HAPPENS ONCE I DEMAND MY EDUCATION?

Notes & Questions:

Expose Hypocrisy / File A Grievance / Be Honorable

Chapter Six: Don't Accept No

Reflect & Answer:

How willing you are to negotiate supports your honorable character – under what circumstances should you refuse anything less than what you are demanding?

_____
_____
_____
_____
_____
_____
_____
_____
_____
_____
_____
_____
_____
_____

How likely is it that you could make it this far on this journey without the support of others?

_____
_____
_____
_____
_____
_____
_____
_____
_____
_____
_____
_____
_____

CHAPTER SIX:
Wrap-Up Questions

What does it mean to "Expose Hypocrisy?"

_____
_____
_____
_____
_____
_____
_____
_____

What does it mean to "File A Grievance?"

_____
_____
_____
_____
_____
_____
_____
_____

What does it mean to "Be Honorable?"

_____
_____
_____
_____
_____
_____
_____
_____

Expose Hypocrisy / File A Grievance / Be Honorable

CHAPTER SEVEN:
CALL FOR BACKUP

When I tell you to *Call for Backup*, I am asking you to **Petition and Appeal** to a team of righteous authority figures who are willing and able to support you. Partnering with them allows them to work toward a desired end greater than what is possible for you alone. Being connected to them is a commitment that allows their influence to defend and protect you while you are in a position of weakness. Trusting in and depending on them instantly connects their anxious position of standby to your humble vulnerability. To call on the willingness and ability of this team to actively support you, you must know, understand, and embrace these principles:

1) Allow Advocacy
    Accept that requesting and depending on others to commit their power, authority, and resources to you is the only way to avoid reaching your limits and unavoidably failing.

2) Honor the Agreement
    Communicate honestly and consistently, stay properly positioned and loyal to the alliance, and show appreciation to prompt an ally's refusal to allow you to be left weak and vulnerable.

3) Plead the 5th
    Stop all interactions and conversation immediately if an individual makes you feel weak, unheard, or unsafe and request the presence of an ally.

MORAL OF THE STORY

Notes & Questions:

Reflect & Answer:
What purpose does the story serve in introducing this chapter?

Allow Advocacy / Honor the Agreement / Plead the 5th

WHO ARE MY ALLIES?

Notes & Questions:

Allow Advocacy / Honor the Agreement / Plead the 5th

Reflect & Answer:

How difficult is it for you to ask for help – what are you trying to get over or battling against when trying to decide if you are going to ask for help or not?
_____
_____
_____
_____
_____
_____
_____

Do you know who your allies are currently – how do they advocate for you – what are the terms of these alliances?
_____
_____
_____
_____
_____
_____
_____

What areas of your life are you most likely to need the influence of others to be successful – what are you doing/going to do to get allies for these areas?
_____
_____
_____
_____
_____
_____
_____

Allow Advocacy / Honor the Agreement / Plead the 5th

ALLY STRENGTH ASSESSMENT & PLEDGE

As a student seriously pursuing an education, it should be fairly easy to find allies. Maintaining student integrity puts you in the right position to attract such assistance. However, you want to make sure that you partner yourself with individuals who are dependable, capable, and have influence that you do not. Thus, finding allies and forming alliances is really going to be based on your ability to assess potential strength and communicate the progress of your pursuit with the people closest to you:

1) Can I trust this person to advocate for me?
2) Can I depend on this person to advocate for me?
3) What interest does this person have in seeing me achieve my goal?
4) What influence (authority/power/resources) does this person have that I do not?
5) What influence (authority/power/resources) is this person willing to make available to me?
6) Does my relationship with this person allow for honest and consistent communication?
7) Is this person aware of how much of a commitment it is to be an ally for me?
8) Is this person dedicated to the responsibility of being my ally?
9) How likely is it that I succeed in accomplishing my goal with this person as my ally?
10) How strong would an alliance with this person be based on the answers provided?

I acknowledge that I understand the importance of attaining and sustaining allies by committing to and maintaining the relationship we have and the allied agreement that we commit to. I appreciate my ally's commitment and contribution to my success, and I will not take it lightly.

_____(Signature)

Allow Advocacy / Honor the Agreement / Plead the 5th

HOW DO I FORM A STRONG ALLIANCE?

Notes & Questions:

Allow Advocacy / Honor the Agreement / Plead the 5th

Reflect & Answer:

How strong of an ally does your influence allow you to be for others?

_____
_____
_____
_____
_____
_____
_____
_____
_____

Do you, and those closest to you, know enough about each other's goals to support each other as allies?

_____
_____
_____
_____
_____
_____
_____
_____
_____

What is the true quality of the relationships you have developed?

_____
_____
_____
_____
_____
_____
_____

Allow Advocacy / Honor the Agreement / Plead the 5th

HOW WILL MY ALLIES BE THERE FOR ME?

Notes & Questions:

_____

Allow Advocacy / Honor the Agreement / Plead the 5th

Reflect & Answer:

Can you think of a time when you ran out of power, authority, or a resource and needed that of another to kick in automatically – how much of a relief would that have been in that situation?

Have you ever had/wanted/needed someone to fight for you?

Allow Advocacy / Honor the Agreement / Plead the 5th

HOW DO I NOT ACCEPT NO?

Notes & Questions:

Allow Advocacy / Honor the Agreement / Plead the 5th

Chapter Seven: Call For Backup

Reflect & Answer:

Have you ever allowed those who were wrong to be right simply because you did not want to "fight" with them anymore – what message does this send about the validity of your position?

What concern of yours should the treatment of others in society be?

Do you have the fight and resilience that it will take to acquire an education?

Allow Advocacy / Honor the Agreement / Plead the 5th

KNOW NOT TO ACCEPT NO CHECKLIST

Having someone tell you no when you have made a righteous request is illegal. No, it is not an *actual* crime, but there is no other way for you to look at it. It simply cannot be allowed. Perhaps it discourages you from asking the same individual again. Maybe it could even delay the honoring of your request. Nevertheless, it is never acceptable to let a "no" response be the end of your demand. You accepting a no is especially wrong if you can confirm these facts:

1) I am a student.

2) I have maintained the character and integrity of a student.

3) My request is in alignment with the promises of righteous, educational authorities.

4) My power, authority, and resources were right to be used in making this demand.

5) My allies, and the terms of our alliance, support me in making this demand.

CHAPTER SEVEN:
Wrap-Up Questions

What does it mean to "Allow Advocacy?"

What does it mean to "Honor the Agreement?"

What does it mean to "Plead the 5th?"

Allow Advocacy / Honor the Agreement / Plead the 5th

CONCLUSION:
YOU OWE YOURSELF

When I tell you, *You Owe Yourself*, I am challenging you to hold yourself **Accountable** for knowing, understanding, and embracing the role, responsibility, and obligation of a student. To be a student is to always be ready and equally prepared for the pursuit of an education. To be a student is to actively explore and experience the educational opportunities you are exposed to with an open mind and curiosity. To be a student is to use the seat of a child as an incubation chamber for the next phase of life. To assist yourself through the educational process of life, know, understand, and embrace these principles:

1) Gear Up:
    There are integral thoughts, supported by corresponding actions, that reveal a distinct character for an individual who is actively engaged in the pursuit of an education; possess and prove these things to be the foundation of your identity.

2) Grow:
    Ask questions to explore the possibility of your curiosity, take advantage of opportunities to attain knowledge and understanding, and make ignorance and inexperience irrelevant in your existence.

3) Go:
    Attain the power and permission to claim your education and be empowered to approach and enter adulthood with the clarity, preparation, and confidence necessary to live a successful, fulfilled life.

WHAT DO I OWE MYSELF?

Notes & Questions:

Reflect & Answer:

What other information do you think is important for you to have to better understand what "go to school and get an education" means?

_____
_____
_____
_____
_____
_____
_____

What do you think is different between those that choose to perform a function and those who look to fulfill a purpose?

_____
_____
_____
_____
_____
_____
_____
_____
_____

What would you offer the world if your power, authority, and resources were unlimited?

_____
_____
_____
_____
_____
_____
_____
_____
_____

CONCLUSION:
Wrap-Up Questions

What does it mean to "Gear Up?"

_____
_____
_____
_____
_____
_____
_____
_____

What does it mean to "Grow?"

_____
_____
_____
_____
_____
_____
_____
_____

What does it mean to "Go?"

_____
_____
_____
_____
_____
_____
_____
_____

Gear Up / Grow / Go

CONCLUSION:
Wrap-Up Questions

What does it mean to "Demand It?"

_____
_____
_____
_____
_____
_____
_____
_____
_____
_____
_____
_____
_____
_____
_____
_____
_____
_____
_____
_____
_____
_____
_____
_____

"Power concedes nothing without a demand. It never did and it never will. Find out just what any people will quietly submit to and you have found out the exact measure of injustice and wrong which will be imposed upon them, and these will continue till they are resisted with either words or blows, or with both."

Frederick Douglas

Gear Up / Grow / Go

GLOSSARY OF TERMS

Accountable – being anchored by and firmly attached to an obligation or responsibility.

Active Participant – student persona resembling a permissive readiness to observe the instruction of educational leadership energetically and optimistically in hopes of acquiring a high-quality education.

Adolescence – a transitional phase, between childhood and adulthood, where one's ability to prove they can control and be responsible for their life, by doing things appropriately and efficiently with a high probability of success, allows those with partial control and responsibility for their life and livelihood to give up control and responsibility fully.

Adolescent – one who has attained limited control and responsibility for their life and livelihood because of increased learning, understanding, maturing, education in the study of life, and the limited ability to do things appropriately and efficiently with a good probability of success.

Adult – one who has attained full control and responsibility for their life and livelihood because of superior learning, understanding, maturing, education in the study of life, and the ability to do things appropriately and efficiently with a high probability of success.

Adulthood – a phase of life after adolescence where superior learning, understanding, maturing, education in the study of life, and the ability to do things appropriately and efficiently with a high probability of success allow one to have full control and responsibility for their life and livelihood.

Advocate – the recognition of a position of weakness and vulnerability paired with an offering of supportive actions meant to defend and protect.

Ally – an individual, entity, or institution that has a joint interest and agrees to partner with another in their pursuit of a goal.

Authority – having the permission or being in the position to deny or grant the allowance of using power.

Caregiver – one who is focused on fulfilling the basic needs of a child.

Certified – considered to be educated by an officially authorized governing body or agency in a particular area or field of study.

Child – one whose life and livelihood are the responsibility of another more than they are for themself, because of their need for learning, understanding, maturing, and an education in the study of life.

Childhood – a transitional phase in a child's life, before adolescence, where the exploration of curiosity leads to learning, understanding, maturing, and an education in the study of life that prompts those responsible for their life and livelihood to give them limited control and responsibility over their own life.

136 – Glossary of Terms

Classroom Management – a teacher's ability to assess how well the academic environment provides space and opportunity for the exposure to, exploration of, and experience with an education, and steer experiences away from low levels of effectiveness while pushing toward higher levels.

Demand – to make an official request from a position of authority and refuse to be denied.

Discipline – the process of putting someone under control.

Education – a unique assortment of information that one possesses, understands, knows how to use, and benefits from (qualitatively).

Educate – to take the lead in a focused effort to assist students in their pursuit of an education.

Educated – possessing qualitative evidence of an acquired education.

Educator – one who, intentionally, teaches lessons and plans activities that allow students to be exposed to, explore, and experience an education to provoke and support them in pursuing and acquiring an education.

Educational Value Continuum™ – a scale that documents and expresses how one could use and benefit from a variety of functions and possibilities contained within academic information once that content has been possessed and understood.

Know the Word / Memorize the Definition / Embrace the Meaning

Engaged Agent – student persona embodying an acute preparation to adhere to the educational process eagerly and expectantly with aspirations of acquiring full mastery of the educational possibility.

Fun – enjoyment of an experience.

Graduate – one who is ready, prepared, and qualified for an advanced educational level by becoming certified as a successful student on the previous learning level.

Grievance – a specific complaint filed with righteous authority for the purpose of solving a problem.

Hypocrisy – professing a standard or belief that one's character or behavior fails to support.

Influence – the persuasive energy of one's power, authority, and/or resources that act on or prompt another.

Integrity – having thoughts, words, and actions that all resemble the same thing.

Intense Trainer – educator persona exemplifying astute intuition while demonstrating supreme proficiency and mastery of a high-quality education.

Know the Word / Memorize the Definition / Embrace the Meaning

Miseducation of Education™ – an endemic issue plaguing the education system caused by a failure to explicitly define "education," which produces and perpetuates obstructions to the productivity, possibility, and promise of the system: disallowing any assurance that progression through an institution's academic program is purposed for acquiring an education.

Noble – held and regarded in a class or rank esteemed highly above others because of one's distinguished excellence.

Parent – one who takes responsibility for a child's life, livelihood, growth, and development while providing safe, appropriate space and opportunity for that child to explore their curiosity while becoming more knowledgeable and experienced in areas where learning, understanding, and maturing are necessary.

Power – the ability to do.

Prepared – fulfillment of the internal and external prerequisites necessary to accomplish a thing.

Profound Mentor – educator persona exhibiting keen insight while demonstrating practical integration of a high-quality education.

Pupil – one who is willing to submit to instruction and participate in learning.

Qualified – possessing educational abilities and evidence that project and predict probable success.

Know the Word / Memorize the Definition / Embrace the Meaning

Ready – acknowledgment of an internal desire and willingness to accomplish a thing.

Righteous Authority – being properly positioned with and connected to a higher source of authority and, thereby, permitted to allow or deny the usage of power to those dependent upon you.

School – a designated area that provides space and opportunity to be exposed to, explore, and experience an education.

Student – one who actively engages in the pursuit of an education.

Success – the achievement/accomplishment of one's goal(s).

Teaching – the utilization of knowledgeable lessons and/or activities to instruct an intellectual minor in an academic discipline, practical ability, or vocational skill set.

Teacher – one who provides an intellectual minor with an understanding of knowledge previously unfamiliar through teaching.

ABOUT THE AUTHOR

Daniel C. Manley is an American educator, author, speaker, and educational provocateur who has made it his life's work to make the attainment of a high-quality education a real possibility for all young people. As a mentor, teacher, and administrator, he has served the middle school and high school population for nearly twenty years. As Co-Founder and CEO of Stand & Withstand Integrity Group, he has made it his mission to empower and prepare children to be firmly planted, deeply rooted, and properly positioned as adults with an education that allows for them to achieve practical success.

Coming Soon
SUPPLY IT:
What "Teaching Is A Noble Profession" Really Means

USE IT & BENEFIT:
Functions & Possibilities of an Education Series

For Booking
Stand & Withstand Integrity Group LLC
P.O. Box 782771
Wichita, KS 67278

CONTACT@STANDWITHSTAND.ORG

www.ingramcontent.com/pod-product-compliance
Lightning Source LLC
Chambersburg PA
CBHW070044120526
44589CB00035B/2309